zero to
STUDIO

Nicola Cartan

Nicola Cantan is a piano teacher, author, blogger and creator of imaginative and engaging teaching resources from Dublin, Ireland. She loves getting piano students learning through laughter and exploring the diverse world of music making through improvisation, composition and games.

Nicola's membership site, *Vibrant Music Teaching*, is helping teachers all over the world to include more games and off-bench activities in their lessons so that their students giggle their way through music theory and make faster progress.

Nicola also runs a popular blog, *Colourful Keys*, where she shares creative ideas and teaching strategies, and hosts regular training events for piano teachers.

Zero to Studio

Nicola Cantan

Colourful Keys Books

Copyright © 2024 by Nicola Cantan

All rights reserved. This book or any portion thereof may not be reproduced or used in any manner whatsoever without the express written permission of the publisher except for the use of brief quotations in a book review.

Published in the Republic of Ireland

First Printing, 2024

ISBN 978-1-913000-37-0

Colourful Keys
78 Durrow Road
Dublin, D12 V3A3

www.vibrantmusicteaching.com

*To my younger self, who had no idea
the wonder that was in store when
she sent out those first flyers.*

Contents

Lesson 0: Prepare 1

Lesson 1: Place 3

Lesson 2: Price 7

Lesson 3: Policies 14

Lesson 4: Promotion 21

Lesson 5: Pedagogy 25

Lesson 6: Planning lessons 30

Lesson 7: Practice 34

Lesson 8: Parents 38

Lesson 9: Preschoolers, Teenagers & Adults 46

Lesson 10: Power 52

Lesson 11: Performances 57

Lesson 12: Profit 62

Bon Voyage! 67

Acknowledgements 69

More from Nicola Cantan 70

lesson zero: prepare

Lesson 0
Prepare

Take a deep breath.

You're about to begin your journey into one of the best careers on the planet. Being an independent music teacher is immensely rewarding and can provide you with a solid and steady income. But starting out can be confusing and overwhelming.

All the information you'll find in this book can be found on the internet in one way or another. What I'm here to do is to distil all the noise into a digestible format that gives you just what you need to get going.

So, please, stop trawling through social media videos and endless tabs on your browser. Just for the length of this book. It's short (as I'm sure you've noticed), so just stick with me, and we'll get all the basics sorted.

As you read, make sure to fill out your Zero to Studio worksheets. These will help you further refine the information and give you an action plan to take you from zero…to studio. (Imagine that!) You can find these at vibrantmusicteaching.com/zerotostudio.

Once you're done with this book, and you've got your studio up and running, you can return to the swarm of ideas on the internet. They should seem less overwhelming once you've got this foundation in place.

Now, a quick note about my assumptions about you:

- I'm presuming you can already play your instrument very well.
- You may or may not have a music degree, but you have had some formal outside assessment of your playing.
- You are interested in teaching as a career and are serious about doing it well.

As long as you meet these criteria, I can help you get your studio off to a great start. So, let's dive in and get you up and running.

🌴 *lesson one: place* 🌴

Lesson 1
Place

Step 1 is to decide where you will teach. You may have a simple answer to this question like, "The purpose-built, piano-shaped castle attached to my house." If that describes you, then feel free to skip this part. Go on, jump to lesson 2 right now.

Now that those lucky ducks have left us, let's talk about the possible locations for your teaching studio.

YOUR HOME

You don't have to have a piano castle to teach from your home. You don't even need to have a room to spare. You can teach from the corner of your living room if that's where your piano is. The main consideration is how this will fit in with your life and the lives of anyone who lives with you. It won't work to have your brother/husband/girlfriend/roommate watching TV in the same open-plan space where you're teaching.

If you do have a space that is manageable, just double-check that you're allowed to teach from home where you are, as well. Homeowners associations or local government regulations sometimes restrict this.

STUDENTS' HOMES

Many teachers commute to students' homes to teach. Parents love this service as it's one less activity that they have to chauffeur their kiddo to.

There are challenges with at-home lessons, though, especially when it comes to the setup. Make sure you have a meeting with the parents before you start lessons. At this meeting, you can ensure that the piano is in a location in the home that can be closed off during lesson times. Otherwise you'll be competing for students' attention and find it very challenging to teach them. If it is a playroom, see if they can put away the toys or hide them before the lesson. If it's in the living room, make sure there won't be fights with the older brother who wants to play video games at the same time.

I'd also recommend talking to the parents about the time directly before the student's lesson. They need to make sure that the child is in a good frame of mind at the start of the lesson time. That means no screens or other highly engrossing tasks for 10-15 minutes before you arrive. If the arrival of their piano teacher means interrupting their game or being forced to take a break from their art project – that's not a good recipe for a successful lesson.

Finally, you'll need a good system for your own stuff. When I travelled to students' homes, I had a folder for each student. I put everything I planned to use in that student's lesson in that folder when I was preparing for the week. Then, when I was about to leave for the day of teaching, I would just grab all the folders for that day and know I had everything I needed. I also kept a backup game, pencil case and stickers in my bag at all times.

ONLINE

Many teachers started teaching online during the COVID-19 pandemic. A small portion of those teachers decided that they wanted to keep teaching online for the long term. From my perspective, the results of this have been a mixed bag. There are benefits for the teacher of teaching online such as being location-independent, avoiding commuting and being able to use technology to teach in different ways.

The benefit many expected, though, is a two-headed beast: Marketing. While it seems logical to think that teaching online could make marketing easier, that's not always so. Yes, you can reach students anywhere in the world, and you can take advantage of time zones to teach at different times of the day.

However, you are limited to those students and parents who are open to online lessons. Those students also have a choice of a teacher from anywhere in the world.

So you're casting a wider net – but it has much bigger holes in it. If you live in an area where the cost of living is high, that's going to price you out of the budget of those who live in lower-income areas. If you want to be a 100% online teacher, you'll need a teaching specialty that makes you stand out and a solid marketing plan for your niche.

RENTED LOCATION

If none of the above options will work, you can look into renting a teaching space. This is easier in some areas than others. You likely won't be able to afford a commercial space when you're just starting out. But if you can find a church or school that will rent out a room to you, that can be a great option.

lesson two: price

Lesson 2
Price

We're ripping the band-aid off nice and early. **It's time to talk about money.**

Pricing is an emotional issue. Anyone who tells you they have a simple formula for pricing a service is barking up the wrong tree. Is it logical that you're more likely to buy something that's 9.99 than 10? Nope. But humans aren't that logical.

SETTING YOUR FEES

So if there's no secret formula, we need to do some digging. Start by looking up the other teachers in your area. Do some search-engine sleuthing and see if you can find out what their fees are.

If you have a local music teachers' association, joining may make this research easier. You can also look at our industry report at colourfulkeys.ie/report to get an idea of rates in your area.

Additionally, it can be helpful to look at other kids' activities and tutoring services. Just be careful that you're comparing like with like. The fees for a 30-children dance class really have no bearing on one-on-one music lesson fees.

Once you have some kind of benchmark in your area, you might be tempted to go a few dollars below the lowest rates. After all, you are a new teacher, right? If you're less experienced, surely your lessons should be cheaper?

This is a mistake.

Undercutting the market is not the route to success. First of all, if you're the cheapest, you're going to attract the parents who are looking for the cheapest. These bargain-hunters tend to quibble about policies, argue about getting every penny they're "owed" and are likely to jump ship whenever you raise your rates. Secondly, those who are not looking based on price will wonder what's wrong with you. They'll think your lessons are somehow less valuable than the other teachers in your area.

I recommend going roughly at the high end of the middle. Or, if there are only 1-2 teachers in the area, try to match their rates.

TRAVEL FEES

If you're going to teach in students' homes, please make sure you are paid for your travel time. In the beginning, that time doesn't seem like a big deal. But once your studio fills up, you'll start to resent the time you spend in the car/on the bike/bus/scooter/ferry/spaceship because you could be teaching more lovely students from your waiting list and bringing in more income.

In my studio, we only take at-home students within a 5k radius. They pay the equivalent of about 25 minutes extra per week for this service. They only pay this extra fee for the first student. So if there are 3 siblings taking lessons back-to-back, they'll pay the at-home rate for one student, and then the regular rate (what we charge for lessons here at the studio) for the 2 other students. This is just an example, and it may not be right for you. (If you live in a high-traffic neighbourhood, you may need to charge for a lot more than 25 minutes!) Just please don't omit the travel fee. You need to be paid for your time.

FLAT FEES

Charging a flat monthly or semesterly fee means that your clients are paying the same amount each month/semester for being a part of your studio.

>Lesson rate x lessons per teaching year
>÷ months per teaching year

We have a calculator for this at colourfulkeys.ie/rates if you don't want to do the maths.

This fee is based on the number of lessons in the year but it remains the same whether there are 2 lessons in a month or 5. A flat monthly fee can also factor in other benefits of your studio such as group workshops, recitals, lending libraries, prizes or any other goodies.

When you use a flat fee system, you never tell parents or students your per lesson rate. You're only using that to calculate your fees for each month or semester. This encourages your clients not to think of getting every minute and every second of what they paid for. They're paying to be part of your teaching studio – not for exactly 30 minutes every week.

It also makes it easier on parents. When I first started teaching at age 15, I charged €12 per lesson (shockingly low, even then) and parents had to find the exact change each week. When I switched to payments for the whole term, the parents were so relieved to be able to just write a cheque.

PRORATION

A quick note on proration, since I get this question a lot. If you charge a flat fee, what do you do if people start part way through the year?

The answer: You prorate the first month or the first semester. Some teachers find this a little confusing, so I'll walk through the steps slowly. Try putting in fictional numbers as you go so you can see how it works.

Let's say the student is starting in the second week of November and your year runs September – June. The first step is to work out how many lessons are left in the year. Then multiply this by the per lesson rate to get the total amount they should pay for the rest of the year.

Lessons remaining in the year x Per lesson rate = Total amount due

Now, there are still seven months left (December – June) in the year where they're going to pay you the regular monthly rate. So multiply your regular rate by seven.

Full months remaining x Regular monthly rate = What they will pay

Then take this away from the amount they should be paying for the year and you'll get the amount they should pay in November when they start.

Total amount due - What they will pay = First month fee

If you're bewildered please don't stress. This may seem a little complex when laid out like this in words, but if you plug your studio numbers in, you'll get the hang of it.

RATE RAISES

Once you finally decide on your price, you might be tempted to leave it and avoid thinking about it ever again. Money can be an uncomfortable topic, and we don't like confronting it more often than we have to.

But if you do leave your fees the same, you're giving yourself a pay cut each year. Inflation means that your dollar, euro or rupee can buy less over time. So if you don't at least increase your rates up to the rate of inflation, you'll effectively be making less.

When you're first starting out, this may not seem like a big deal. So, you make a little less next year, so what? If you raised your rates you might lose clients, and that would be far worse for a growing studio… right?

The thing is, as much as teachers fear it, parents probably won't quit your studio if you put your fees up a tiny bit. And if you do it every year, that's all it will need to be – just a little bit.

Raising your rates once a year also trains them to expect this. They're a lot less likely to baulk if this happens regularly than if you leave it for 5 years and then suddenly jump up to a much higher rate.

So make it a habit. Look up your local inflation rate and increase your fees at least that much every year. I recommend doing it either over the summer break or at the New Year. Then send out the new rates to

lesson two: price

parents in your studio in the most matter-of-fact way you can manage. No apology or justification is required. Keep it simple! For example, "Here are the new fees and calendar for the next academic year. Register before the 12th of Forever to secure your place for the next term."

Lesson 3
Policies

Having a set of policies for your studio will help you avoid so many headaches down the road. The word "policies" may sound a bit scary, and possibly gives the impression you'll be getting a lawyer involved, but they really can be simple. You just need to lay out on paper the basic rules of how you'll run your studio.

I believe in keeping policies short and to the point, no more than one page. They don't need to cover every possible eventuality, just the main things.

You can download a sample set of policies (and other useful studio paperwork templates to make your teaching life easier) at vibrantmusicteaching.com/zerotostudio *lesson three: policies*

PAYMENT METHODS

When and how will people pay you? The "when" is the easy part to answer. They should be paying *before* they receive the lessons. So for monthly payments they'll pay at the end of the month for the following month. For semester payments they'll pay before the semester starts.

The "how" is more dependent on where you are in the world. Your basic payment method options are cash, cheque, bank transfers and cards. Where I am, in Ireland, everyone uses internet banking and setting up a direct bank transfer is very easy to do. If that's the case for you too, I recommend this option. It's hassle-free for you and them, and it's the cheapest.

If you do want to accept cash or cheques, make sure everyone gives it to you in an envelope clearly marked with the student name and date they're giving it to you. Trust me, at the beginning it's easy to remember who gave you what and when – but it gets a lot harder as you get more students and the months blend together in your mind.

Finally we have card options and payment apps. For these, you will end up paying a fee. You can use a free invoicing service like Wave or a music-teacher specific management tool like My Music Staff or Fons. These websites may not charge you for the transactions – but the payment processor will. That might be worth it to you; you'll just have to factor it into your fees. If you're planning to use an app like Revolut, Zelle,

Venmo or similar, just check their terms of service. On most of these platforms, you are required to set up a specific business account and it may have fees attached.

LATE PAYMENTS

What counts as a late payment? And is there any penalty for paying late? If you've decided folks will be paying you for the following month by the end of the previous month, perhaps it counts as "late" straight away on the 1st. Most teachers introduce a little leeway or a grace period before actually adding on a late fee. The most common policy I have seen is to add 10% late fee added 5 days after the invoice is due.

If you use an online invoicing system, you can often have this late fee add on automatically. This makes it easier for you to actually follow through on this policy because it feels like someone else (a computer) is being the bad guy.

CALENDAR

In most communities, it makes sense to follow the same calendar as the local schools. Parents expect after-school activities to take the same breaks as their school does so that they can plan vacations and day trips at those times. You will likely know what the expectation is in your area, but if you don't, take a look at the calendar information for other local kids' activities like sports, dance and art classes.

lesson three: policies

Put together a simple calendar that clearly shows your weeks off (I like to mark them in grey) so that parents can see at a glance when the lesson breaks are. You can also put special studio events like recitals or group workshops on the calendar, too. You can see a sample calendar at vibrantmusicteaching.com/zerotostudio.

If you decide to use studio management software like My Music Staff or similar, input the breaks there as well. You should also list them on your studio website and put reminders when they're coming up on your social media. Yes, that's a lot of places but we're trying to minimise the amount of individual emails and texts you answer about whether lessons are on or off each week!

Having your calendar fully set out is not just good for parents – it's great for you too. I've known many teachers who will schedule lessons for 50 weeks out of the year. This isn't realistic for you or your studio families. We all need on and off seasons and, anyway, some of the weeks you have off from lessons won't be time off at all – they'll be spent doing office work, lesson planning and research. So make sure you have enough breaks in your teaching calendar that you get some real vacation time.

MISSED LESSONS AND LATENESS

I recommend making this extremely clear cut: no makeups, no reschedules. If a student has to miss a lesson, you can offer a video lesson where they send you a video in advance and you review it during the lesson and provide feedback. I do this with our practice app, Vivid Practice.

I'm trying to give simple, succinct answers here but if you want to hear me ranting about why I don't believe in makeup lessons, do an online search. There's plenty there to dive into. :)

In the case of inclement weather or other unpredictable situations (hello, pandemic!) lessons will go online. Make it clear in your policies that this isn't their choice. They can't choose to get a refund if there's a snow day and you need to teach your lessons online.

Lateness should be handled differently depending on lesson location. If you're teaching at students' homes, I recommend a policy of calling or texting and then waiting for 5 minutes if they're not at home. That way, you're not stuck in the rain or cold and can go get a coffee before your next lesson, or go home if it's the end of the day.

If your students come to you, just make it clear that the lesson will still finish at the scheduled time. Even if they're 25 minutes late for a 30-minute lesson, you can listen to one piece and give them some quick feedback. Don't get in the habit of giving them extra time even if you feel like you don't mind at that moment. It might not seem like a big deal in the moment but, unfortunately, this will just increase the chance they're late again. You need them to respect your time.

TEACHER ABSENCES

Any time I bring up no makeup lesson policies, someone asks about teacher absences. Am I saying you shouldn't make those up either?

Of course not. Teacher absences are a completely different story because it's you that can't show up at the agreed-upon time. There are a few different ways to handle this but my favourite is to allow for a couple of absences by charging for fewer weeks than you schedule. You can then explain in your policies that two (or whatever number you choose) teacher absences have been accounted for, and if you have to miss any more lessons, you will refund or put a credit on their next payment.

If it happens that you don't use these two teacher absences during the year, you'll just finish two weeks early. Don't try to explain this in your policies. Unless someone asks, wait until it actually happens to explain it.

Chances are, you will have a couple of weeks you have to miss due to illness, emergencies or events like weddings and funerals. Allowing for these in advance means you won't feel conflicted or guilty taking that time off.

PHOTO AND VIDEO PERMISSIONS

I don't recommend putting this in with the rest of the policies, but it does need to be covered somewhere.

Give the parents an option, either at the bottom of the policies or on the enrolment form, to say yes or no to photos or videos of their child in lessons being used on your website and social media. It's useful to get this in writing right from the get-go.

It might be tempting to lump it in with the rest of the policies and say that by enrolling in your studio, they give you consent to take photos and videos and post them online. However, this is bundled consent and in an increasing number of countries it is against the law. I'm not saying the police are actually going to chase you down for it, but think of it this way: Do you really want a parent to be turned off from your studio just because you insist on sharing photos of their child? I personally don't want that to be a deal breaker for joining my studio.

POLICY TALK

This section has been about the written policies. While it is important to lay these things out on paper, the most important part is what you say and do. Parents are barely going to look at these rules – and they're certainly not going to refer back to them later. It will be your job to explain the policies to them verbally when they join your studio (more on this in the 'Parents' section) and to follow your own rules.

You can change them, but don't bend or break your policies or they won't be worth the cost of the ink.

lesson four: promotion

Lesson 4
Promotion

Enough with the setup; we need to get you some students! Marketing/promoting/advertising your studio (whatever you want to call it) can be one of the most frustrating things when you're first starting out. If you ask an established teacher what works for them, they will usually (enthusiastically) say, "word of mouth!"…not great advice when you don't yet have any students to refer other students.

The marketing techniques that work will vary a lot based on where you are. So in this chapter, I'll give you a few suggestions that work for many teachers. Try one tactic at a time and don't get disheartened if you don't see instant results. You will find something that successfully brings in new students if you're patient and persistent.

WEBSITE

Setting up a website is a great first step if you're pretty sure you want to give this teaching thing a real shot. These days, you really don't need to be super technical to set one up, either. If you're willing to put in a little time, you can get a website up and running without paying hefty fees.

You can use a website builder like Wix, Weebly or Squarespace if you prefer. These come at a bit of a premium but many find them more user-friendly. Personally, I prefer a self-hosted Wordpress site as it gives you more control, and can generally be better optimised for search engines. If you want a step-by-step tutorial on how to do that, you can find a course on setting up a studio website inside Vibrant Music Teaching.

Whatever way you set it up, here are the basic pages you need on your site:

- Home
- About
- Lesson info
- Contact

That's about it. Call them different names if you like, but try to keep it simple. Make sure your writing is neither too dense nor too sparse. You want to give enough information that parents (and search algorithms) get a good idea of who you are and what you do, but no big walls of academically-written text, please! The tone should be friendly and conversational, speaking directly to your potential clients.

GOOGLE BUSINESS

Alongside your website, Google Business is your best friend for getting found online. Try searching for something local right now, e.g. "dance class San Antonio" and you'll see the map listings right at the top of the page. You need to set up Google Business to have a shot at appearing there. Once you have a few clients, you should ask them to leave a review on your Google Business page, too, to increase your chances of getting to the top of these listings.

SOCIAL MEDIA

I think it's worth setting up social media accounts for your studio and joining local groups that allow promotion. Just don't place too much stock in them bringing in new students. You may get some enquiries through social channels but most studios don't. However, I still recommend setting them up as many potential parents will look you up on Instagram or Facebook, just to get more context after seeing your website. Plus, they can be a good way to strengthen the community in your studio once you have a few students.

FLYERS AND LEAFLETS

Don't rule out print media completely! This can be a bit hit or miss as most people do tend to search online these days. Still, you never know, and it's a relatively cheap way to advertise your studio locally. Just set up a simple flyer using Canva (or any other design software you like) and post it on library bulletin boards, community notice boards or anywhere else you're allowed to stick it up.

LISTING SITES

General listing sites like Yelp, Gumtree, Craig's List, etc. have mostly faded from popularity. They're not the first place most people go when searching for a service. However, many of these listings are free so I say, what have you got to lose?! Just don't pay any of them for a premium listing as it's usually not worth it.

CONNECTIONS

Now we come back to the word-of-mouth arena. Even if you don't have students yet, you can still use your connections to try to get new students simply by telling everyone about your new teaching business. Don't be shy! Tell your family, friends, people you meet, friendly dogs…anyone who will listen. You never know who knows a friend of a friend who's looking for a teacher.

Once you have a few students, make sure you encourage them to pass on your name, too. Sometimes all people need is a little nudge to tell their friend. Maybe that friend will tell 2 of their friends and, before you know it, you'll be overflowing with a waiting list.

lesson five: pedagogy

Lesson 5
Pedagogy

A reminder that the aim of this book is just to get you started on your teaching journey. Pedagogy is a vast subject – one you'll keep studying for the rest of your life if you stick at this teaching gig! When you're ready to dive a bit deeper, you can take our full 'Foundations of Piano Teaching' course at vibrantmusicteaching.com/foundations. For now, though, let's get you started with some basics.

METHOD BOOKS

Once you start paying attention to piano teaching blogs, groups, forums and other discussions, you'll hear a lot about method books. Some teachers swear off them completely, some are devoted to a particular series and others (like me) use a variety. What I think gets left out of most of this chatter, though, is how valuable they are for beginner teachers.

That's really why they were designed, after all. An experienced teacher could teach from anything and still cover all the bases and make it interesting for the student. But, as a beginner teacher, it's a great thing to have a method book to hold your hand and ensure you don't miss anything.

I'm not going to recommend any particular method book series here. Here's what I do advise you to do:

- Do some research and pick 3 method books that seem interesting to you.
- Purchase them and start to work your way through. Estimate how much material is meant for one lesson (probably 3-4 pieces) and write some notes about what the student learns/reinforces each week in this method book.
- If you have a willing friend or family member, teach them some of the pieces from the method books so you can see how they respond and what's challenging.
- Play through all the pieces in the book several times. Aim to make even the simplest pieces sound beautiful.

Once you feel you're quite familiar with a certain method book, there's nothing left but to try it with a real student. Keep your teacher copy so you can make notes after you teach each piece about what surprised you, what was challenging and what was easy. Pay

lesson five: pedagogy

particular attention to how reading, technique and artistry are being approached in the method you're using as these are, in large part, what method books are designed to facilitate.

PREEMPT THEORY

Method books can be extremely helpful, but you don't want them to become the teacher. If you are turning the page in the lesson, checking what's on the next page and then explaining it to the student there and then – you're not running the lesson, the book is. To keep control in your hands and help you teach more thoughtfully, try to introduce concepts before they come up in the method book. I call this "preemptive theory".

Sometimes you can preempt the concept with a game, a listening activity or a simple explanation. But aim to introduce each theory element 1-4 weeks before they meet it in their book. That way they can get familiar with the new concept before they're expected to apply it in a piece, and they get more reinforcement to make the knowledge more durable.

INCORPORATE IMPROVISATION

Most method books do not include improvisation. If they do, it's usually pretty minimal and would mean the student is improvising about once every couple of months.

I don't think that's enough.

Personally, I believe students should improvise in pretty much every lesson. I think this is even more essential for beginner students. Improvisation allows students to develop their musicality, technique, expression, sense of rhythm and pulse. This is all easier to do in the context of improvisation because they're not also having to read music at the same time.

We have a lot of different improvisation courses, resources and templates inside Vibrant Music Teaching. But I really want you to see how simple this can be and get started right away.

So, in case you've no experience accompanying improvisation, here's a quick formula:

- Play a I V vi IV progression with your right hand playing the chord and the left hand playing the root note. For example, in G flat major the chords are G flat, D flat, E flat minor and C flat major.
- The student improvises in the matching key. They do not have to use correct scale fingering, they can simply hop from note-to-note.
- Slow down and do a simple V I cadence to finish.

You don't have to be some master jazzer to incorporate improvisation into your lessons! Try this as a warmup at the beginning of each lesson. Start with G flat major (student can just play black keys), then C major and then try other keys as you feel they're ready.

GET MOVING

The final thing that I want to highlight here, mostly because it's something you're unlikely to find in a method book, is movement. Your own piano lessons may have involved sitting on a bench for 30–60 minutes, so you might think that's the only way it can be. But humans (of all ages, but especially children) benefit from moving about a bit. Their concentration and engagement will improve so much if you aim to get them up and moving about often. As a general rule, aim to do a movement activity at least every 10–15 minutes and much more frequently if they're 7 or under.

This movement is not just a brain break. You can use movement to facilitate so much learning. Beginners should be marching to the beat of music and swaying side to side to work on their sense of pulse. All students can do their rhythm practice as body percussion rather than seated clapping drills. You can also use movement as a quick drill of virtually anything by assigning a move or pose to each potential answer. For example, the student has to stretch up tall for high notes and crouch down for low notes, or stomp like an elephant for loud sounds and squeak like a mouse for soft sounds, or jump in the air for the V chord and do a 70s style dance for the I chord. Make these little movement games a regular part of your teaching right from the off, and you'll head off many potential behavioural issues at the pass.

Lesson 6
Planning Lessons

When it comes to improving your teaching, it's all about planning, reflecting and planning again. That's not because you need to have the most amazing plan so suddenly everything will run as smoothly as ice skates and your students will learn 20 times faster…

The reason planning improves your teaching so much is that you can analyse what did and did not work after the lesson. Having a plan written down means that you can assess, improve and iterate. Even if you don't follow the plan to the letter (or something comes up and you need to make a complete u-turn) you will still learn from the planning and reflection process.

TIME ESTIMATES

My favourite type of plan includes time estimates for each lesson component. Something like this:

3 minutes: Improvisation warmup in C major
5 minutes: Practised pieces
2 minutes: March around the room while listening to a new piece, Bumblebee
3 minutes: Play an interval game
5 minutes: Analyse intervals in Bumblebee and practise together
2 minutes: Review scales from last week
5 minutes: Demonstrate new piece, The Detective, and have student try hands separately
5 minutes: Review everything that needs to be practised

This is just a rough outline. In the beginning, you may prefer to make much more detailed notes in your planning process, and then have a quick glance summary to look at during lessons.

If planning takes you a long time in the beginning, please do not despair! It won't be that way forever. Most teachers need a lot of planning time for the first 2–3 years of teaching. After that, you'll be able to streamline your process considerably.

REFLECTION

Make some time after each lesson or before lessons the next day to reflect on how your plans went.

- Did you get everything done?
- Did anything take more or less time than you thought?
- What did the student enjoy most?
- Were there any lightbulb moments for the student?

If you were able to go back in time and redo the lesson, what would you change about your plans or the lesson in general?

After some time reflecting on this lesson, write the plan for the next one. You can then review and alter it before the lesson the following week. If you repeat this process every week, you will go from strength to strength in your teaching.

RECORDING

If you're really committed to becoming a fantastic teacher, recording your lessons is the best way to get there. Videoing all your lessons, watching them back and making notes about what you could do better is the closest thing to a shortcut that you'll find in this profession.

Yes, I know you hate watching yourself and hearing the sound of your own voice. You're not special in that – pretty much every human cringes when they watch themselves. Take it from someone who has recorded thousands of videos of myself at this stage: You'll get over it. The only way to get used to watching yourself is to do it.

lesson six: planning lessons

And it's worth pushing through because there's nothing quite like seeing yourself in action. You may have moments that you thought went pretty well, but you find that the student is actually glazing over during your explanation. There might be other bits that you thought were a gigantic mess but really are just a blip in the overall lesson.

More than anything, watching videos of your teaching will help you to clean up your language. Not from profanity (I hope), but from fluff. We all have phrases we say completely on autopilot that don't really add anything. There's normally a quicker and clearer way to say something than the first one that comes out of our mouths. Watching recordings helps us to refine what we say, and how we say it.

Lesson 7
Practice

With everything in teaching, we need to be aware of our own biases based on our experiences. This is paramount when it comes to practice. Whatever practice looked like in your life has clearly worked out for you, but that doesn't mean it will be right for everyone! Perhaps your parents were very strict about practice or very relaxed, and you're tempted to think that's what all parents should do because it worked well for you. Or maybe you feel you succeeded in spite of the way practice was framed because you took a more circuitous route to the level you're at now.

You are the exception, not the rule.

The very fact that you made it to such a high level of playing means that you are not the norm.

In this chapter, we'll lay out some basics that will help you give your students a good chance of regular practice, and therefore steady progress. Please know that if some of your students do not practise, it does not mean you're a failure. You can try new things and keep iterating over time but practice ups and downs are natural, and most teachers have some students who don't practise at all – they just don't talk about it as openly as they should.

ROUTINE

If you can get your students into a habit of daily practice, it will make an enormous difference to their progress. Giving parents a few tips about how to start this routine will increase their chances. I advise new piano parents to start with tying it to something else that already happens in the day to create an if/then statement. For example, "If we've finished lunch, then it's time to practise." Or, "If we've just got in from school, then it's time to practise."

I'd recommend having this discussion with new parents at your first meeting with them, and then also following up several times, by email and in-person, once they've started lessons. You need to make it clear that it is their responsibility to get practice happening and that their child will have more fun in lessons if they have a steady practice habit.

If you want to go a bit further with practice for parents, you might like to check out my book, Practice Pie, which is written specifically for them.

PRACTICE NOTES

When you start teaching, you may default to whatever practice notes system your teacher used. If they expected you to remember everything you were supposed to do at home, you'll expect that of your students. If they wrote detailed essays in a notebook, maybe you do the same. It's worth taking a fresh look at the options available to you and picking the one that feels right for you as a teacher.

You might choose to go with a digital solution. Many teachers use Google Docs or a dedicated practice app (like our own app, Vivid Practice). This can be a lot more efficient for you as a teacher as you will be able to copy/paste and create templates for assignments. You probably type faster than you handwrite, too, so that speeds things up right away. Also, having digital assignments means you can easily refer back to the notes during your planning process so you don't have to keep two sets of notes.

If you don't want to go digital, you can use a notebook, a binder with assignment sheets or sticky notes stuck all around the music. Think about which makes the most sense to you.

Whichever way you write practice notes, they're only good if students read them! Explain clearly to students and parents what the notes are for, and how they should use them. Keep your notes clear, concise and written in student language so that when they do read them, they're not struck by a tornado of jargon.

PRACTICE STRATEGIES

Once students are beyond the first few months and (hopefully) have a practice routine established, you can shift your focus to how they practise. Teaching simple practice techniques in lessons can make a big difference in your students' practice efficiency.

Make sure to focus on one practice technique for a while and do it at several lessons so they get used to it. Don't just tell them – actually walk through the practice steps together in the lesson. If you do this enough, they will feel confident practising this way at home.

INCENTIVES

A quick and straight-forward note on practice incentives: I don't believe in them. I used incentives as a new teacher and I think many young teachers do, before thinking better of them. Practice charts, rewards and prizes boxes may seem like a good way to get students motivated, but they tend to backfire over time. Students who only practise for the candy tend to resent practice once the candy is taken away. We want the focus to be on how fun it is to get better and play great music, not on what they "get" for putting in their minutes.

Zero to Studio

Lesson 8
Parents

If we want to stay in business, we need to keep our studio parents happy – they're the ones paying the bills. You need to set up systems to ensure that parents are on the same page as you when it comes to their goals for their child, your overall teaching style and lesson expectations.

FIRST MEETINGS

There are many things in this book that were hard-won lessons for me that I want you to learn the easy way. This is one of the most surprisingly important ones: **You must meet with all new parents and adult students BEFORE they start lessons with you.**

Don't start with a trial lesson.

lesson eight: parents

Don't jump straight to regular lessons because it's your grandma's neighbour's friend's kid.

Don't make exceptions.

There are so many issues that crop up when we start lessons without explaining how our studio runs and what our teaching philosophies are. Written communication is not enough because people simply do not read thoroughly. We are all so bombarded and overwhelmed by the amount of content on our screens that we gloss over details and assume we get the gist.

So we have to meet with parents in person or on a video call to avoid misunderstandings. This meeting might only be 10–20 minutes.

Here is a list of things I make sure to cover. I start with a few questions to break the ice and get a bit of chat going, and then I explain some studio basics and practice expectations.

- What's the motivation for starting lessons? Who had the idea first?
- What do they want to get from lessons?
- Did the parents study music?
- What other hobbies does the student have?
- Explain studio policies.
- Give an overview of concerts and other events.
- Explain practice and make sure the parents understand their role.
- Explain my philosophies on exams and my goals for a holistic music education.

Remember, you can download a sample set of policies (and other paperwork templates) at vibrantmusicteaching.com/zerotostudio

From there, they might ask questions of their own. Some parents' only question is, "Great, how do we sign up?". Others will have specific things in mind for their child's lessons and want to further unpack how you do things.

Now, a lot of teachers don't want to do these meetings because they don't want to teach for free. They want to start right away with lessons because their time is valuable, and they don't want to waste it.

This is understandable, but here's the thing: I've had one parent ever (!) that attended one of these meetings and then didn't sign up. That's out of hundreds of students. Before we ever schedule this meeting, I have already emailed back and forth with parents, so they're already pretty committed, and we have a time slot sorted out that works for them.

Here's the other thing: I'm not *teaching* at these meetings. There is no value to them if they do not sign up. I never call it a trial lesson, and we spend no time at the piano. I'm not on trial, and they are not auditioning to be my student, either. This is mainly about policies and practice, not musical ability.

ENROLMENT FORMS

When students join your studio, a simple enrolment

form can streamline the process of collecting their information, and make your studio seem more professional. Create this enrolment form whatever way seems easiest to you. It can be a printed, physical form or a digital one.

The form should have at least these fields:

- Name
- Parent/guardian name(s)
- Address
- Phone number
- Email
- Date of birth
- School grade/class/year
- Special needs, additional needs or allergies

You may also want to include spaces for the student's other hobbies or interests and photo/video consent. (You will need to do further research on what wording is necessary for consent where you live if you do want to include this.)

ANNUAL REGISTRATION

Your annual registration process can be very similar to the initial enrolment process. Most teachers take some kind of summer break so it makes sense to have the registration for the following year happen around then. Give out the registration forms along with the new calendar, policies and fees before the start of your summer break, and require them to be returned to you early in the summer break.

For example, my summer break is in July and August. I give registration information and forms to parents around the beginning of June, and they must return them to me by July 14th to secure their spot for the new year which starts in September. There is a registration fee attached to the form which helps ensure they're committed.

The main difference between my registration form (for returning students) and the enrolment form (for new students) is that the registration form includes availability. That's because I create the timetable for the next academic year during the summer break. I need to know every returning students' availability so that I can give everyone a spot that works for them. (When students are first enrolling, they are filling an open spot, so I don't need availability information.)

Some teachers simply carry over the same timetable from one year to the next and avoid all this scheduling faff. The issue with this is that inevitably, some students will need a different time due to changing schools, new sports practice times or other factors out of their control. If only one or a couple of students need to change times, and everyone else wants to keep their time slot, you're going to have a tough time accommodating these changes. That's why I create the timetable from scratch every year.

This registration process also gives you an easy time to raise your rates or change your policies. If you do not take a summer break, you may choose to do this in the new year instead.

lesson eight: parents

PROGRESS UPDATES

A lot of issues with pushy parents asking for particular pieces or exams before the student is ready can be solved by keeping parents in the loop. The work that happens in music lessons can be largely a mystery to them, and it's difficult for them to see the growth that's happening. Simple progress updates can inform parents about all the fantastic things their child is learning, and how they can help at home.

Our updates are in a table format with 6 categories: Practice, Aural, Rhythm, Reading, Technique and Technical. This helps us to be clear and concise while still informative. Your categories might be different but, no matter what, make sure the language is not full of music jargon. Try to make it understandable whether a parent has any music education or not.

At Colourful Keys, we send out progress updates 3 times a year. If you're just getting started with this, however, I recommend aiming for twice a year. It's easy to underestimate the work involved in this and you can always make it more frequent later on if you wish to.

Not all parents will read these updates in detail but that doesn't mean they're wasted! Filling these out will be useful for you as well. So even if a particular parent never opens their email, writing these notes about their child will be good for your own clarity about their strengths, and the areas you need to focus.

AD HOC UPDATES

Less formal updates have an important place too! Make a point of writing to parents when their child achieves a certain milestone, big or small. Many parents are overwhelmed by email these days so I don't think it's necessary or welcome to email every week. It's more powerful when you write every so often with a fun detail.

NEWSLETTER

Some teachers like to do newsletters every month but personally I prefer just once a year. I'm in regular communication with parents in the studio anyway – my annual newsletter is just an opportunity to sum up our amazing year together, and remind them of all the cool things we did. I send this a week or two before the registration information so that all the positives of piano lessons are top-of-mind when they're considering whether to sign up for another year.

My newsletter always includes features about each event we did during the year like concerts, composing projects and special events. I also write a quick sentence about each of our students' accomplishments. On the back page, I mention what professional development I have done that year and tell them about the exciting things coming the following year.

If you're going to do a newsletter, I highly suggest setting it up at the start of the year (in Canva, Word, Docs or whatever you want to use) and then filling it

lesson eight: parents

out in drips throughout the year. It's a lot less overwhelming than trying to do it all at once.

Lesson 9
Preschoolers, Teenagers & Adults

A lot of the music teaching resources out there assume your student is roughly age 7–12, and many of your students will be in that age bracket. However, it's worth looking at other demographics and being prepared for their unique challenges. This means you'll be ready when they come knocking, and can go into those lessons as confidently as you do all your other lessons.

It also means you can market to these groups specifically, especially if you're having trouble filling your studio. In many areas, these demographics are an underserved market, and could be the key to your breaking through as a new studio. This was the case *lesson nine: preschoolers, teenagers + adults*

for me with preschool students. Marketing myself as a specialist in that age group led to referrals to students of all ages and, eventually, a very full studio with multiple teachers and a waiting list.

When you're marketing yourself as a specialist in preschoolers, teenagers or adults, you better have the teaching skills to back that up so that the word-of-mouth spreads. So let's talk about some of the things you need to prepare for.

PRESCHOOLERS

Real talk, one of my least favourite comments to see from a teacher in an online community is that most students under a certain age are not "ready" for lessons. They're only not ready for lessons if you try to teach them the same way you teach older kiddos. You can have very successful lessons with 4-year-olds, and even 3-year-olds, if you prepare yourself to teach in a developmentally appropriate way.

I have a whole other book, 'Playful Preschool Piano Teaching', that goes into much more detail on how to teach these tiny fingers to play. But here's an overview of some of the key things to look into:

- Patterns that are immediately obvious to adults are not clear to young children. Since music is built on patterns, you need to take time teaching things like the piano keys, finger numbers, rhythms and any other patterns necessary for them to play the music you are working on.

- Get comfortable playing games and making everything you do playful! This is how you will keep them engaged and curious about the concepts you're covering.
- Reading does not need to happen right away and should not be your primary goal. There's so much more to music than reading skills, and your youngest students can benefit much more from a mixture of rote/pattern pieces and ear training with some pre-reading work.
- The parent must take an active role in practice if you're going to expect it. Make this clear from the first conversation with the parents.
- If parents are not interested in working with their child at home, a more general group music class may be a better fit.

OK, that's my best attempt at summarising this topic without making it the subject of *this* whole book! If you do get into teaching the littlest kidlets, please do read 'Playful Preschool Piano Teaching' after you finish this book.

TEENAGERS

Teenagers are a lot more varied. You could have a teenager who has been studying since they were 5 years old or a teenage beginner. They may have goals of going on to study music at university, or they may just want to explore a little bit. Some will only want to learn pop songs, and others might be very serious about Bach. Take each teen as they come and don't make assumptions.

lesson nine: preschoolers, teenagers & adults

The great thing about teenagers is that they're old enough to communicate with you. Sure, it may come out in Gruntish (the universal language of teens in every country) at first, but if you persist, you can get them to open up and develop your lessons based on their goals. Make sure you ask them regularly about their aspirations and any special song requests they have at the moment. You don't have to be up-to-date with what music is cool, they will appreciate your asking and being open to making their favourite songs work when you can.

Apart from being more student-led in terms of goals and repertoire selection, the other big difference with this age-group is that you need buy-in. They will not learn a scale or do their sight reading just because you say so. You need to get them to understand why they're doing this and how it will help towards *their goals*.

And finally, if you get into teaching teens, get ready to ride the practice highs and lows. Many of these students will have a lot on their plate. They may have seasons where they hardly practise at all because they have other things going on in their life. If you learn to make their lessons enjoyable and rewarding even when no practice is happening, your studio can become a safe-haven from the stress.

ADULTS

Finally, we have the adults – the largest grouping in this chapter. Just like teens, adults may come to you with varying levels of experience and different goals for their lessons. One of the things the majority of them have in common, though, is emotional baggage. Many adult students come to us with weighty expectations they place on their own shoulders, and certain feelings they associate with educators and authority figures.

These issues rarely crop up within the first few months of lessons. Initially, they'll be riding high on their excitement at starting something new and probably practise diligently and enthusiastically. If you want them to keep the positivity over the long term, though, you need to have the "guilt chat" early on. From the first lesson, and every so often on an ongoing basis, work into the conversation that you're not there to judge them. Your role is to help them on their musical journey, whether they've practised or not, whether they're struggling or thriving.

Just like with your teenage students, communication without assumptions is essential when teaching adults. Talk with them about their goals, music preferences and how they imagine their lessons looking. Explain the repertoire and other materials you're working on together in terms of how these things move them towards their goals. You don't have to go into great detail, just make it clear that you have carefully thought through your plan for them based on what they want from lessons.

One more quick tip: Try to discourage them from looking at videos of little kids playing virtuosic pieces!

lesson nine: preschoolers, teenagers + adults

If they do come across them, explain how many years of study with daily practice has gone into these young musicians. It's not that children learn like sponges – it's that they've put in the hours!

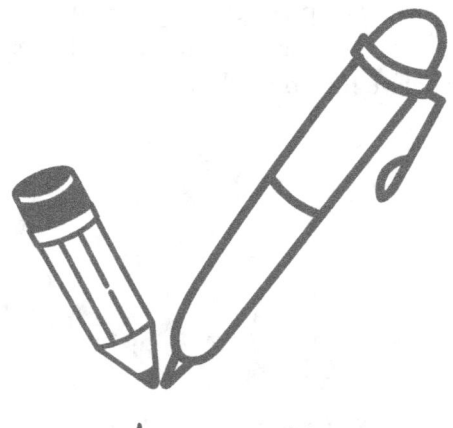

Lesson 10
Power

One of the biggest struggles I see with all the rookie teachers I work with is what you might call the power balance, discipline issues or control of the lesson. I don't like any of these terms, to be honest, but I've gone with 'power' here as it seems the most broad.

In many of your lessons, things will run pretty smoothly even if you give no consideration to the power dynamics. Your students will comply with your instructions, engage with the lesson content and just generally "behave" according to the plan and expectations.

But sometimes it's not that simple. You may have students who have off days, whose parents are making them take lessons, who are neurodivergent and have trouble with your usual approach or who are too young to sit on a bench for as long as you're expecting. You may even have students who just decide they don't really like you and want to push the boundaries.

KEEPING CONTROL

We can head most of these issues off at the pass if we just keep better control of all our lessons. You should feel like you have a command over what's happening in your lessons. It should very rarely get to the stage where your student is refusing to do what you ask, shutting down, doing things you've asked them not to do or interrupting you with their own off-topic talking points.

Being in control of your lessons does not mean that you have to be strict or unyielding. It doesn't mean you never follow students' creative whims or curious questions – that, to me, would be a tragedy.

We want to find the right balance where we feel like we're calling the shots, but we don't feel like a drill sergeant. A large part of this, in my experience, comes down to 2 things:

1. The opening credits
2. The hidden plan

The opening credits is about the very first time you meet a student, and also the start of every lesson. You need to greet your student and welcome them into the teaching room in a way that communicates that you're in charge here. This comes down to subtle body queues like opening the door and gesturing with your arm for them to come in, inviting them to take a seat at the piano and guiding the opening chat.

This is a hard thing to practise at first and may feel a little forced. It may help to think about how a doctor behaves when you walk into their examination room as an example. They don't just let you do whatever you want and strike up a conversation that takes your fancy. They guide you to the right chair and ask what brings you in today. Now think whether the start of your lessons feel similar. We don't want our students to feel as if they're going to the doctor – but we do want them to feel similarly guided and taken care of.

Once we go beyond the opening credits, we communicate to our students that they can continue to be guided by us (and don't need to take over the show) through our hidden plan. This may be based on an actual lesson plan, but it's broader than that. Students sense whether we know where we're going next through our "ums" and "ahs" and the fluffer words we use between different lesson activities.

I'm not saying you're not allowed any uncertainty; I am aware that you're an actual human! Just do your best to think ahead and to guide your student to the next thing. If you're not sure how to word a question or comment, and need a moment to think about it, try a thoughtful silence rather than filling the silence with fluff that makes a student feel uneasy, confused or itching to take control of the situation.

lesson ten: power

DEALING WITH BEHAVIOUR

Building your ability to keep control of the lesson will take time. While that skill is developing, and even when you have mastered it, you will have to deal with students doing things you don't want them to do. Most of the time, students aren't even aware they're doing anything wrong. Sometimes, they're testing a boundary to see whether the same rules apply here as at school or at home. Here's a simple 3-step process to deal with these small behavioural issues as they arise:

1. Explain the rule
2. Summarise the rule
3. One-word reminders

Let's say, for example, that your student is playing their instrument while you're talking. The first time, you might pause and say something like, "When you play while I'm talking, I find it distracting and I'm not sure whether you can hear what I'm saying. Please don't play while I'm speaking. If you want something to do with your hands, you can squeeze this stress ball instead."

The next time, you can simply remind them, "Remember, we don't play while someone is speaking."

And from there on, you can use a one-word or two-word reminder, or even just hold out the stress ball you've suggested they fidget with instead of playing when you're speaking.

This system works for most little issues that crop up in music lessons. It's effective because: It's simple, it gives them a reason for the rule and it provides an alternative behaviour. It also gives them less and less attention each time they do it – as the reminders get shorter each time the behaviour is repeated.

You won't always be able to give them a reason and an alternative, but try to if you can, as many kids will respond better to things they understand. Even if the reason is something like, "No chewing gum in lessons because it's a pet peeve of mine and I find the sound very irritating." (This is an actual rule from my studio – I really just hate gum! Whilst I could've made up some reason that was more generalised to music lessons, I prefer to just be honest. I think my students respect that.)

Now, sometimes, this 3-step process is not enough. Students may push back against your rules, ignore them or just have trouble following them. If you have a student who has significant behavioural issues in lessons, and is doing things that are beyond the scope of what you can deal with, I suggest you discuss the issues with the parent and have them sit in on the lessons so they can see what's happening first hand.

lesson eleven: performances

Lesson 11
Performances

Depending on the part of the world you grew up in and took lessons in, you may have had regular recitals, exams or both in your own music education. Whether they seem like the "default" to you or not, it's worth looking at these performance opportunities, and how they might fit into your music studio.

RECITALS

Putting on a studio recital can be a wonderfully motivating thing for your students. It's also an opportunity for parents in your studio to show up and cheer for their child's musical progress, in the same way they do every couple of weeks for sports. Why shouldn't music parents get to celebrate their kiddos just like the soccer parents do?

Many new teachers are intimidated by the idea of putting on a recital but it doesn't have to be so big and scary. There is planning involved, yes, but it doesn't have to be a huge production unless you want it to be.

Start with deciding on the venue. If you only have a few students, you may be able to do it in your regular teaching space or living room. Some teachers ask parents to volunteer to host the recital at their home if they don't have a space big enough. If neither of those will work, look at local churches, community halls, schools and small concert venues. Ask around, and you can hopefully find a space that's affordable.

Once you decide on your venue, you'll need to set your recital date. If there are multiple dates that could work for you and your venue, put out a simple survey (e.g. a Google Form) to your studio families and ask them to mark all the ones that they could attend. Let them know that you'll go with the majority. (Don't try to please everyone! That's a recipe for frustration and potential resentment if they back out later after you move the date for them.)

Now you get to start preparing your students for the recital. At least for your first recital (and potentially for all of them) don't give your students specific challenging recital pieces. Just pick one of the pieces they already know and help them polish it to performance standard. If you're going about it this way, you can start the preparation about 6 weeks before. Have them start every lesson from that point forward

lesson eleven: performances

with a run through of their recital piece or pieces. Get them to:

- Sit away from the piano (as if they're in the audience)
- Walk up to the piano and sit down with their hands in their lap
- Play their piece, keeping going even if they make mistakes
- Put their hands back in their lap
- Get up, smile and take a bow
- Walk back to their seat

This takes more drilling than you might imagine but it's worth it to get students used to the performance routine and build their confidence.

During these preparation weeks, you should also explain to them what the recital will be like, and describe the scene so they can imagine it fully. This will really help with managing their nerves.

Closer to the big day, you can make a program and print it out. (Don't do this too far in advance as there will be last-minute changes and absences!) I like to have my students follow the program and go up when it's their turn, I don't announce each performance.

After you host your first recital, give yourself a huge pat on the back…then maybe start planning the date for your next one. You'll be hooked before you know it.

EXAMS

Now, again, depending on where you're based, music exams may be a foreign concept to you. If that's the case, I recommend tabling this issue for a few years. You can look into exams – and where they might fit into your studio – once you have a few years of teaching under your belt.

But in many parts of the world (including Ireland where I live), exams are expected as part of music lessons. If that's the case where you live, you need to decide where you stand on them, and start the discussion proactively with the parents from the first meeting. Otherwise, you'll be left on the back foot when parent expectations don't align with your plans.

Personally, I prefer exams to be an occasional extra, not a default. I make it clear to parents right away that:

- No student does an exam for the first 3 years of study
- Transfer students can't do an exam until they've been with us at least 2 years
- We will suggest an exam when we think it would be beneficial to the student
- Exams are never obligatory, and there's no pressure from us
- Students may have on/off exam years, e.g. sitting grade 3 and then nothing for a few years and then grade 6

lesson eleven: performances

This is the balance that works for me. You'll likely need to experiment and sit with this for a while before you land on the approach that works best for you, so don't put too much pressure on yourself to make these decisions right away.

Lesson 12
Profit

Too many teachers end up turning a blind eye to their finances (save maybe getting an accountant to sort it out in a panic at tax time) and then wonder how they're working so hard and can barely rub 2 cents together.

There is no secret to this stuff. You don't need incredible maths or business acumen to run a profitable studio. You just need to look the numbers in the eye and do a little planning.

WORK BACKWARDS

We need to start from the result you want. So, how much do you want to make? This can be a tricky question to answer. Take your time and add up all

lesson twelve: profit

your expenses. Some of the expenses will be basic and necessary like groceries, utilities, rent or mortgage payments, car maintenance, etc. Others will be more optional but important to you and your lifestyle like gym memberships, zoo passes, theatre tickets and brunches in swanky restaurants. Do your best to estimate how much you spend and what you spend it on each month.

Now, check your work. Take out your bank account statements and add up the amount you spent under the different categories for 3 different months. Does it match with your estimates? Square the numbers with each other, and then continue.

If you haven't already included some savings in your budget, I suggest you add that now. If you're going to be self-employed or run a small business, you're going to have to plan for your retirement and save for big purchases. Increase the amount at least 10% to add a savings cushion.

Next, you need to reverse engineer your taxes. You should be able to find a calculator online so you can work out the gross pay from the take-home pay.

All of this will give you the minimum amount you need to make with your current lifestyle. We're going to work backwards from there.

- Take the annual amount you need to earn (if you worked out the monthly amount just multiply by 12).

- Add at least 10% for studio expenses – more if you know you have big fixed costs like a commercial space. We'll call this your gross income.
- Work out how many weeks you'll be teaching in the year. *Reminder: It should not be anywhere close to 52! You need time off and there are likely weeks in the year when most families in your community won't want lessons.*
- Divide the gross income by the number of weeks.
- Now divide this weekly figure by the number of students you want to have.

What's left is the amount you should be charging students per lesson. (We're not going to charge them per lesson, but it's good to know what this amount is.) Work out your flat fee from the per-lesson fee, as discussed in our 'Lesson 2: Price'. Does this match, or come close to the pricing you decided on previously?

If it is the same or comes pretty close, then you're golden. You can move forward knowing that your aspirations and your business model match up nicely.

If not, you have 5 things you can do:

1. Increase your fees
2. Change your lesson format to groups or hybrid lessons to get more from your time
3. Increase the number of students you're willing to take (please be careful with this; if you push it too far it's a surefire recipe for burnout!)

lesson twelve: profit

4. Reduce your studio expenses
5. Reduce your personal and lifestyle expenses

Play around with the numbers and these levers until the jigsaw fits together. Do not put your hands in your ears, sing the Spring theme to yourself and hope it will all fix itself. You'll only be kicking the problem down the road to your future self and she's a cool person! Don't do that to her.

BEFRIEND SPREADSHEETS

The second part of this chapter is more comfortable for most, but hard to maintain in the long run. You need to stay on top of your studio numbers on an ongoing basis. Set up a system now that you can use to log expenses and income so that you always know where you're at. You can use spreadsheets, a general accounting program like Wave, Quickbooks or Xero, or one specific to music teaching like My Music Staff or Fons. This makes tax season easier, but you're not doing it *because* you have to for taxes, OK? You're doing it because you want to know what's happening in your business.

While you're at it, make sure you have a separate bank account that is for your business and do not mix this up with your personal account. If you're buying something for your business, always use the business account. If it's not a business expense, always use your personal account. No exceptions!

Finally, you need to find your rhythm with keeping

this up-to-date. Just like getting a practice routine going, this can be hard in the beginning. Set alarms on your phone or a physical calendar on your fridge. Whatever you need to do to establish a habit of updating your bookkeeping and taking the business of your music teaching business seriously.

Bon Voyage!

Congratulations on completing this book. Now, all that remains is for you to go out there and take action. You absolutely will make some mistakes and missteps as you get your studio going – that's only natural. Please don't chastise yourself when you need to make changes and make sure you reach out to the teaching community if you need help troubleshooting. Remember, if you'd like more resources and a video course to cover the concepts in this book, you can find that at vibrantmusicteaching.com/zerotostudio. You can also join our Vibrant Music Teaching membership when you're ready for lots more resources, courses and support.

Acknowledgements

I will be forever grateful to my piano teacher, Eimear, who suggested I start teaching when I was just 15 years old. I'm not sure she was right that I was "ready" (I sure wish I'd had this book, or at least non-dial-up internet!) but it has led to the most wonderful and fulfilling career.

Thanks to team VMT for editing and proofreading this book, especially Sarah and Carmen for being endlessly patient with my misplaced commas. I could not do this work I love so much without the incredible teachers on our team.

Finally, and most importantly, to you dear reader. You are the next generation of music teachers. You are going to keep this train of music-making growing and, eventually, pass on your wisdom to future the generation after you. I hope this book helped you on your journey.

More from Nicola Cantan

Thank you for reading *Zero to Studio*. If you liked the book, please leave a review wherever you purchased it. I'd truly appreciate it.

Go to vibrantmusicteaching.com/zerotostudio to get your free templates. And if you're interested in more teaching resources, you might also like these.

Vibrant Music Teaching

Vibrant Music Teaching is the perfect resource to help you level-up your lessons and teach using more creativity. There is a library of video courses and every printable game and activity you could need for your students. To get more information and sign up for membership, go to vibrantmusicteaching.com.

Thinking Theory Books

Thinking Theory is a series of music theory workbooks designed to accelerate learning while providing plenty of reinforcement of each concept. Everything is presented in a clear and concise way and no topic is introduced without being revisited several times later in the book. The workbooks incorporate solfa singing and rhythm work. Take a look at thinkingtheorybooks.com.

Colourful Keys Blog

I write regular articles and share ideas on my blog, *Colourful Keys*. Check it out if you're looking for more piano teaching inspiration: colourfulkeys.com.

The Piano Practice Physician's Handbook

We all know a huge amount of the learning that needs to occur happens in the practice room, not the lesson room. This book (specifically for piano teachers, although many of the ideas can be adapted) will help you to help your students practise more effectively.

Playful Preschool Piano Teaching

Preschoolers need to move, sing and explore. They need to PLAY. In this book, I've broken down the most effective teaching strategies for preschool piano.

Rhythm in 5

Many piano students struggle with rhythm, but it's hard to fit in extra rhythm work – and even harder to make it fun. *Rhythm in 5* helps teachers do that with movement and improvisation.

www.ingramcontent.com/pod-product-compliance
Lightning Source LLC
Chambersburg PA
CBHW072105110526
44590CB00018B/3328